CHOOSE A CAREER ADVENTURE

SUPER BOWL

K. C. Kelley

Created and produced by
Bright Futures Press, Cary, North Carolina
www.brightfuturespress.com

Published by
Cherry Lake Publishing, Ann Arbor, Michigan
www.cherrylakepublishing.com

Photo Credits: cover, Shutterstock/Eugene Onischenko; page 5, Shutterstock/Media Union; page 5, Shutterstock/katjen; page 5, Shutterstock/Mark Herreid; page 7, U.S. Air Force; page 8, Shutterstock/Dmitry Fokin; page 9, Shutterstock/bikeriderlondon; page 9, Shutterstock/Phase4Studios; page, 11, Atlanta Falcons; page 13, Shutterstock/Extreme Sports Photos; page 13, Shutterstock/mts aride; page 15, Shutterstock/Eugene Onischenko; page 17, Shutterstock/Michael Staniewski; page 17, Shutterstock/Michael Decher; page 19, Shutterstock/Zerbor; page 21, Shutterstock/Syda Productions; page 21, Shutterstock/Local Favorite Photography; page 23, istock/stevecoleimages; page 25, Shutterstock/IxMaster; page 25, Shutterstock/igor.stevanovic; page 27, Shutterstock/antb; page 29, Shutterstock/Brocreative; page 29, Shutterstock/Eugene Onischenko.

Library of Congress Cataloging-in-Publication Date

CIP has been filed and is available at catalog.loc.gov.

Printed in the United States of America.

CHOOSE A CAREER ADVENTURE

SUPER BOWL

Let the Games Begin!

Every year, the most-watched live-televised sports event in America is the Super Bowl. More than 100 million people tune in to see which team will win the championship of the **National Football League** (NFL).

The two opposing teams' players are the stars of the ultimate showdown, of course, each led by its starting **quarterback** and a **head coach**. But hundreds of other people play key roles in bringing the blitz into fans' homes while showcasing the top two teams of the NFL.

Sports trainers help keep the football players in top physical condition, while reporters and announcers give fans the inside scoop on what's happening on the field and behind the scenes. The game is played in four fifteen-minute **quarters**—which can last up to twice that in "football minutes" with timeouts and commercials. After the second quarter, a creative show producer puts on a **halftime extravaganza** of music and color that's almost as much fun as the game.

Do you have what it takes to be a part of this championship event? Read on to find out and let your Super Bowl career adventures begin!

TABLE OF CONTENTS

HALFTIME SHOW PRODUCER

Go to **www.youtube.com** and search for "Super Bowl Halftime Shows."

Producer needed for short but very important d widely-watched song-and-dance extravaganza during halftime of the Super Bowl. Should be creative, quick-thinking, and very, very organized. Interest in music, dance, and performance a must. Ditto on the ability to inspire people who work with you. Knowing how to have fun is a big plus!

- ***Ready to take on this challenge?***
  Turn to page 6.
- ***Want to explore a career as a Head Coach instead?***
  Go to page 9.
- ***Rather consider other choices?***
  Return to page 4.

Super Stars

The Super Bowl is more than just a football game. It's an entertainment super event! Some fans tune in to the broadcast just to watch the halftime show. Over the years, it has included some of the biggest names in music: Michael Jackson, Bruce Springsteen, The Rolling Stones, Beyoncé, Madonna, The Who, Coldplay, and many more. Your job as the **halftime show producer** is to make it spectacular. There is no room for mistakes. After all, millions of people are watching!

The first step is to sign up the musical acts. It's an honor to be asked to play in this show. Only the biggest names of the moment get asked. Your job is to work with them to plan a short playlist and to design the show. You work with other creative people to design, light, and **choreograph** the action. You work for weeks, planning every step of every second.

You also have to spend time talking to reporters, who want to know all you can reveal about the spectacle. For you, Super Week is super busy!

Five Thousand Feet

This isn't about measurements! Your Super Bowl halftime show includes more than 2,500 people swarming over the field. Count 'em up. That's 5,000 feet—get it?

You have to make sure all the dancers, extras, and technicians know where to be at every single moment. It's like a giant jigsaw puzzle, but with all the parts moving around! The dancers are all volunteers. But if you do your job, and they do theirs, fans in the stands and at home get an incredible show.

Timing is Everything

The entire show takes place within 12 minutes. That leaves just enough time for the stage to be set up and then taken down when the music is over. You have everything timed to the millisecond.

Just like that, the stage is ready. You give the **cue**, and it's showtime! Rock on, everybody!

You count down the seconds as the music plays, and then it ends! In moments, you make sure the huge stage vanishes from the field. After that, you can settle back and enjoy the final two **quarters** of the game. Your job is over! Enjoy the game!

Your Halftime Show Producer Career Adventure Starts Here

EXPLORE IT!

Use your Internet research skills to find out more about the following:

Who performed in some of the very first halftime shows? Hint: these shows have come a long way in representing pop culture.

Pull out your crystal ball to see if you can name five performers who should be asked to perform at the next Super Bowl.

With so much diversity, how has the halftime show represented all kinds of music? Go back to the past shows, and rate the performances.

TRY IT!

Rock On!

It's your turn to pick the music! Choose your favorite musical artists, and make up a playlist for their halftime show. Remember, they only have 12 minutes, so you have to find out how long each song is and pick the very best ones.

More Than Just the Music

Katy Perry rode in on a giant mechanical elephant. Diana Ross landed on the field in a helicopter. What wild-and-crazy entrance can you come up with for the halftime show? You can make a sketch or a video, or just write about it.

HEAD COACH

Head coach wanted for NFL team with one goal: make it to the Super Bowl. High-pressure position with endless amounts of stress. Must answer to the team's owner and fans—none of whom like the team to lose. Deep knowledge of football and the ability to work with all-star players and rookies essential. Must be a leader players will follow into battle!

- ***Ready to take on this challenge?***
  Turn to page 10.
- ***Want to explore a career as a Quarterback instead?***
  Go to page 13.
- ***Rather consider other choices?***
  Return to page 4.

Find out what it's like to interview for an NFL head-coaching position at **http://bit.ly/HeadCoachInterview**.

No Excuses

You are an NFL head coach, a job that only 32 people can have at one time (that's how many NFL teams there are!). And you are one of two head coaches preparing to face off at the Super Bowl championship game this year.

If your team wins, you'll be praised as a genius. If the players make mistakes and your team loses, it will be viewed as your fault—even though you didn't even touch a football. It's a difficult job. But you've been preparing for this game your entire life. Bring it on!

In Demand

Even though your players only practice for about two hours each day, your workdays during Super Bowl Week are, oh, about 24 hours long. There is so much to do! You spend hours watching videos of your opponent's best moves and more hours watching videos of your team's previous games. You gather information and make a list of plays to run.

Then there are all the meetings. You are always in demand. You meet with assistant coaches and talk with the quarterback. You have to prepare the team and strategize. You have to motivate your players and also keep them on track with all the national attention. There are NFL **press conferences**, where you and the other team's head coach are expected to speak.

Game Day

When it's time to take the field, you make one final speech. This is your last chance to inspire your team, to convince them they can win no matter what. Some coaches shout and yell, but that's not your style. You are bold and **assertive**—determined to say whatever it takes to motivate your players and make this a winning day.

As the game begins, you watch every play intensely. You communicate via a radio headset with coaches in booths high above the field. They can see more than you, so they provide key information. You are in charge of calling **timeouts** and talking with game officials as well as keeping other coaches and the players levelheaded.

As the game winds down, your team is ahead. All that hard work paid off. There is just one more job: stand still while your team pours ice-cold Gatorade over your head. It's a victory ritual and you love it!

Your Head Coach Career Adventure Starts Here

EXPLORE IT!

Use your Internet research skills to find more about the following:

The most inspiring NFL locker room speeches

The different types of assistant football coaches

The best Super Bowl coaches of all time

TRY IT!

Get Your Team Ready!

Choosing the plays is just one small part of a coach's job. Another key part is helping players get better. Invite your team over for a backyard game. As the coach, you cue into their strengths and help build their confidence. Teaching is your aim. If, for example, someone is coming up short on running a certain drill, you might offer up direction on how they can do it better. Encourage! Encourage! Encourage!

Psych 'em Up!

Before the Super Bowl, the coach has the last word before players hit the field. Write up a short talk that you can give to them. How will you use your words? Will you tell them how great they are? Or how proud you are? Write a speech that would make you want to go out and win!

QUARTERBACK

Quarterback needed to lead team to Super Bowl championship. Must be able to pass football accurately and carry it while being threatened by monster-size tacklers. Strong leader with the courage to make tough calls preferred. Willingness to do everything necessary to lead team to victory required.

- ***Ready to take on this challenge?***
  Turn to page 14.
- ***Want to explore a career as a Sports Journalist instead?***
  Go to page 17.
- ***Rather consider other choices?***
  Return to page 4.

Check out the history of the Super Bowl at **www.nfl.com/superbowl/50**.

High Five

Your team has made it to the Super Bowl. Now the pressure is really on. You are the team's **quarterback**. Your team and all its fans are counting on you to bring home the win!

You work with coaches and teammates to make a game plan for the Super Bowl. A big part of that involves studying your opponents. You have to find ways to beat them. Is their defense strong against the pass game? Then your speedy **running backs** should be putting in extra work.

As the quarterback, you control the offense while on the field. You have to be able to "read" the opposing team's defense—that is, how are they lining up? You may have to "audible"—change the play at the line of **scrimmage**—to keep them on their toes. You also have to watch out for those gnarly **linebackers**, who are looking for that illustrious sack. (A "sack" is when the quarterback gets tackled behind the line of scrimmage.) So you really need to look alive while holding onto that **pigskin**!

Game Face

The big day finally arrives, and you run out onto the football field through a tunnel that leads from the stadium's locker rooms. The sound of the crowd is deafening! More than 60,000 people are screaming their heads off. It's like being in the bottom of a bowl of noise! But that noise is fuel. It pumps you up and puts you in your zone.

You are firing on all cylinders! You are confident in your team and making plays. The scoreboard reflects that. But the other team is relentless. They aren't going away. You exchange **touchdowns**, and the score is tied with less than a minute to play.

You are one good drive away from victory. You throw downfield a couple times and gain 40 yards. But you are 35 away from the **uprights** with only seconds left on the game clock.

You take the **snap**, drop back, and eye up your **receiver**, who is making his way to the end zone. You release a bullet to him just before you feel the ferocity of a linebacker taking you down.

You don't see the catch, but you hear the crowd scream and feel the ground shake.

You're flattened under 250 pounds of linebacker, but it doesn't matter. The only thing you feel is ecstasy. You are a Super Bowl champion!

Your Quarterback Career Adventure Starts Here

EXPLORE IT!

Use your Internet research skills to find more about the following:

The history of the Super Bowl

The best Super Bowl quarterbacks of all time

Football players who have won the most MVP awards

TRY IT!

Name Your Dream Team

A quarterback can succeed only with help from teammates. As you get ready for *your* Super Bowl, make a list of friends or family you'd like to huddle up with. Or pick an all-star team of real-life NFL stars to help you score the coveted Super Bowl ring!

Super Speech-Maker!

What if you were to win the Super Bowl? How awesome would that be?! Part of winning the game means you'll be expected to chat it up with sports reporters and your fans. Pretend you're a Super Bowl-winning quarterback. Write up a short speech you'd make after winning the Super Bowl MVP award.

SPORTS REPORTER

Sports reporter wanted to cover the Super Bowl for major sports website. Should be excellent writer, with great command of football language and **sports statistics**. Ability to write very fast required, plus the skills to ask anyone questions—even if they're sad after losing.

- ***Ready to take on this challenge?***
  Turn to page 18.
- ***Want to explore a career as a Sports Trainer instead?***
  Go to page 21.
- ***Rather consider other choices?***
  Return to page 4.

Find out what it is like to be a Super Bowl reporter at **http://bit.ly/SuperBowlWriters**.

Your Big Game

Grab your digital recorder and laptop—you're going to the Super Bowl! You aren't playing in the game, you're reporting on it. A major sports website has chosen you to be live on the scene of the big game, and its editors want you to write a steady series of reports. It's up to you to sniff out the best stories.

Thousands of members of the media—TV, websites, newspapers, and more—pour into every Super Bowl city. You'll be competing against all of them for news and stories. It's your own version of "playing the game." The NFL makes the players and coaches available at crowded press conferences. You'll write a new story every day based on the information you get from the players.

Get the Scoop

At the Super Bowl, you sit in the press box high above the field. It's actually a pretty good view. And just look at all that free food! As you watch the game, you take lots of notes. You listen to the crowd react. You watch players on the sidelines. You see how coaches and trainers engage, all while watching the game on the field. The NFL provides all the reporters with tons of stats and trivia, so you pay attention as it's your job to weave what you see and what you hear into a story of the game.

Super-duper Deadline

As soon as the game ends, you head into a designated area for press conferences. Locker rooms are usually closed to the media right after the game unless you are part of the network broadcast. Once you're in the press area, you conduct interviews with key players from both teams. You try to find out what they were thinking and feeling during the game, and how they are reacting to winning...or losing.

After the interviews, you race back to the press box. While other reporters work noisily around you, you somehow type 800 perfect words about the game. After a quick read-through, you hit "send."

It's been a real whirlwind, but now you know that perhaps millions of people will read about this game—and they'll read words written by you! Who knew a job could be this exciting!

Your Super Bowl Sports Reporter Career Adventure Starts Here

EXPLORE IT!

Use your Internet research skills to find more about the following:

News stories about past Super Bowls, starting with Super Bowl I

Sports writers who have covered the most Super Bowls—some have been to 40 or more of the "big games"

Big sports news websites like ESPN (www.espn.com) and Sports Illustrated for Kids (www.sikids.com)

TRY IT!

Go Deep!

Find a friend, and have him or her pretend to be the Super Bowl-winning quarterback. Conduct an interview, asking questions about the game and about his or her career. Remember, you have to try to find a story idea that's unique and different from those of other reporters.

Writers Gotta Write!

Next time you watch a football game—even if it's not the Super Bowl—write a news story about the game. Write up something that could appear on a website or in a local newspaper. Make sure to say who won, who lost, what the score was, and what the biggest plays were. Try to make it as nearly as entertaining as watching the game live!

SPORTS TRAINER

Read about a Green Bay Packers trainer at **http://bit.ly/GreenBayTrainer**.

Trainer needed to work with Super Bowl-bound team, to keep players healthy and ready to play. Duties include running warmups, wrapping body parts with tape, and caring for injuries that happen during games and practices. Should be able to think on your feet, react calmly in a crisis, and be ready for just about anything! Background in sports medicine required.

- ***Ready to take on this challenge?***
  Turn to page 22.
- ***Want to explore a career as a TV Announcer instead?***
  Go to page 25.
- ***Rather consider other choices?***
  Return to page 4.

Ouch

Football is a tough, physical game. Players need to be in top shape to play. Sometimes—often—players get hurt at practice or during games. As the trainer, you're part of both sides of that deal. You work hard to keep players physically fit, and you patch them up when they are injured.

Pregame Prep

On Super Bowl Sunday, your workday begins long before the players arrive. You're at the stadium at the break of dawn, making sure your medical supplies are ready to go. You fill a small pack with first-aid gear, which you keep with you throughout the game. You also check that the ice machine is working—football teams go through hundreds of pounds per game to ice up injuries.

As players arrive, you begin to tape ankles, wrists, and knees. Some NFL teams use more than 80 miles of tape during a season! The strong tape helps keep their joints safe during the games. This work goes on until the game's **kickoff**.

As the game moves on, a big part of your job is making sure your staff keeps players hydrated. That means having water and sports drinks available at all times. You also help players with any minor scrapes or cuts they get. You probably even have to retape an ankle or two!

When the cornerback goes down hard after tackling the other team's receiver, he can't make it off the field on his own. You are the first one on the scene, rushing to his side. You quickly assess the injury, waving over the rescue staff and a stretcher to carry the player to the locker room for care.

Halftime Is Go Time

While the rest of the world enjoys the halftime show, you are busier than ever. The players fill the locker room, and you work like a bee in a hive. Moving from player to player, you pass out water and apply ice bags, bandages, and, yes, more tape!

When your team wins, you celebrate...but only for a moment. After a game, players need even more treatment. Some players need ice baths, while others need heating pads, depending on the nature of the injury. Your victory party starts after you have taken care of every player on the team.

Your Sports Trainer Career Adventure Starts Here

EXPLORE IT!

Use your Internet research skills to find more about the following:

What kind of training sports trainers need in order to become certified

The most common sport-related injuries football trainers have to address

What an NFL trainer's day-to-day job looks like during off-season

TRY IT!

That's a Wrap

Find an online video about how to wrap an ankle. Every trainer has to do this quickly and perfectly. It's not as easy as it looks when it's all done! Try it out on a friend.

Train Yourself

NFL athletes' conditioning is pretty intense. Not only do they work out with weight machines, but they also do calisthenics to build strength, as well as stretching to get warmed up and cool down. By the time they get to be in the NFL, they are usually regimented and disciplined with their workouts. Can you relate? What kinds of exercise do you enjoy? Try everything to pinpoint things you love. That way your conditioning won't be a chore but a nice way to escape!

TV ANNOUNCER

USA Today ranked the best Super Bowl announcers ever: **http://bit.ly/SuperBowlBestandWorst**.

Announcer needed to broadcast the biggest sports event in the country! Must have deep knowledge of football and ability to describe plays quickly and clearly. Time spent studying the game and its players long before kickoff required. Strong and powerful voice essential. Looking confident on camera a must.

- ***Ready to take on this challenge?***
  Turn to page 26.
- ***Want to explore a career as a Halftime Show Producer instead?***
  Go to page 5.
- ***Rather consider other choices?***
  Return to page 4.

Good Afternoon, America

The minute the two teams in the Super Bowl are known, your work as a Super Bowl announcer begins. You study each team carefully, reading stats and biographies of all the players. You watch videos of past games and meet with network experts about what to expect in the game.

As the game gets closer, there are many more meetings. The announcer is only one of hundreds of people working on the TV **broadcast**. The crew includes producers, directors, camera operators, editors, graphics experts, and engineers of many kinds. The TV network pays tens of millions of dollars to air this game, so they want its broadcast to be perfect!

Totally Teamwork

Your best skill is talking rapidly and clearly, but you've never played in the NFL. That's where your partner comes in. Most Super Bowl announcing teams include an expert "analyst" who is a longtime NFL veteran. These former football players know what it feels like to make a tackle, get hit, or score a big touchdown. They also understand the strategy and plays on the field. As the main announcer, you need to work with your partner as a smooth-operating tag team.

You make sure to get a good night's sleep on Saturday night. On the morning of the game, you take special care of your voice. You drink some hot lemon water and do some vocal exercises. At the stadium, you go into a makeup trailer. For part of the game, your face is on TV, so you want to look your best. You also wear the TV network's logo on your jacket—a production assistant helps make sure you're dressed perfectly. You gather up a stack of notes and stats, which you'll need during the game.

Last thing before the camera's red light goes on? Go to the bathroom! No breaks for you until halftime!

Shout Out!

Once the game begins, your job is to tell 100 million fans what is going on—play-by-play, call-by-call. You wear a headset so a director can feed information to you, even while you're talking to fans! As the game gets more and more exciting, you can't help bubbling over with enthusiasm. You love this game!

Your TV Announcer Career Adventure Starts Here

EXPLORE IT!

Use your Internet research skills to find more about the following:

Great plays in Super Bowl history

Famous Super Bowl announcers

Television announcer training

TRY IT!

Get Your Lips Ready!

You can't be tongue-tied when millions of people are listening. Just like athletes, announcers have to warm up. Read about some "vocal exercises" and try them out. Some of them can sound a bit weird, so you will probably want to do them in the privacy of your own room!

Get Ready for Your Speech!

The next time you watch a football game on TV, turn off the sound. You are now the announcer! Describe the plays and action you see, as vividly as you can. For extra fun, use a cell phone or other recording device to record yourself. It's not as easy as the people on television make it seem, is it? Practice makes perfect!

WRITE YOUR OWN CAREER ADVENTURE

WRITE YOUR OWN CAREER ADVENTURE

You just read about five six awesome Super Bowl careers:

- Halftime show producer
- Head coach
- Quarterback
- Sports reporter
- Sports trainer
- TV announcer

Which is your favorite? Pick one, and imagine what it would be like to do that job. Now write your own career adventure!

Go online to download free activity sheets at www.cherrylakepublishing.com/activities.

ATTENTION, ADVENTURERS!

Please do NOT write in this book if it is not yours. Use a separate piece of paper.

GLOSSARY

assertive having or showing a confident personality

blitz in football, attack the passer in a blitz

broadcast to send out to a wide network; available over the air so that cable is not needed

choreograph to design a dance or a musical performance

drive series of offensive plays

extravaganza elaborate and spectacular entertainment or production

halftime time at which half of a game or contest is completed, especially when marked by an intermission

halftime show producer person who organizes entertainment during football games

head coach highest ranking coach of a coaching staff

interceptions passes thrown by the offense that are caught by the defense instead

kickoff football game to be started or resumed by a player kicking the ball from a designated spot

linebacker defensive football player normally positioned behind the line of scrimmage

line of scrimmage imaginary line where the offense and defense line up before each play

media people who report news for TV, radio, newspapers, websites, and more

MVP trophy honor bestowed on the best-performing player in an entire league, for a particular competition, or on a specific team

National Football League (NFL) major professional football league in the U.S.

pigskin football

press conference an event at which people take questions from a gathering of media people

quarter segment of a football game, of which there are four in every game; in the NFL, each quarter is fifteen minutes long

quarterback football player positioned behind the center who directs a team's offensive play

receiver offensive player in football who is also eligible to receive forward passes

running back offensive player in football who specializes in carrying the ball

snap backward pass from the center to the quarterback to start each play

sports reporter person who writes reports about sporting events for newspapers, magazines, websites, and more

sports statistics collection of data about the performance of an athlete or sports team

sports trainer highly trained health care who provides prevention, evaluation, treatment, and rehabilitation of athletic injuries

time out short period of time during a sports event when the game stops and the players rest or talk to their coach

touchdown six-point score made by carrying or passing the football into the end zone of the opposing side, or by recovering it there following a fumble or blocked kick

TV announcer person who describes and comments on the action in a broadcast sports event

uprights goalpost

INDEX

ABOUT THE AUTHOR

K. C. Kelley has published dozens of books for young readers, mostly about sports. He is a former sports journalist who has written about the Summer and Winter Olympics, among other big sporting events.